Focus on Climate Change

CLIMATE CHANGE MODIFICATIONS

How We Are Adapting

KAYLA ANDRA

TWENTY-FIRST CENTURY BOOKS / MINNEAPOLIS

For Alan, Andre, Anthony, Erica, Cash, and Paige.

Twenty-First Century Books™
An imprint of Lerner Publishing Group, Inc.
241 First Avenue North
Minneapolis, MN 55401 USA

For reading levels and more information, look up this title at www.lernerbooks.com.

Main body text set in Bembo Std Regular.
Typeface provided by Monotype Typography.

Library of Congress Cataloging-in-Publication Data

Names: Andra, Kayla author
Title: Climate change modifications : how we are adapting / Kayla Andra.
Description: Minneapolis, MN : Twenty-First Century Books, [2026] | Series: Focus on climate change | Includes bibliographical references and index. | Audience: Ages 11–18 | Audience: Grades 7–9 | Summary: "Climate change impacts all life on Earth. Many groups and individuals will have to adapt to survive. Learn what adaptation means, how it's measured, the ways groups are already adapting and might in the future, and more"—Provided by publisher.
Identifiers: LCCN 2025011152 (print) | LCCN 2025011153 (ebook) | ISBN 9798765644201 library binding | ISBN 9798348029579 paperback | ISBN 9798348000066 epub
Subjects: LCSH: Climatic changes—Juvenile literature | Climatic changes—Effect of human beings on—Juvenile literature | Adjustment (Psychology)—Juvenile literature
Classification: LCC QC981.8.C5 A53 2026 (print) | LCC QC981.8.C5 (ebook) | DDC 304.2/8—dc23/eng/20250604

LC record available at https://lccn.loc.gov/2025011152
LC ebook record available at https://lccn.loc.gov/2025011153

Manufactured in the United States of America
1-1012702-52446-5/5/2025

CONTENTS

INTRODUCTION — 4

CHAPTER ONE
MEASURING ADAPTATION — 9

CHAPTER TWO
CHALLENGES OF ADAPTATION — 19

CHAPTER THREE
ENVIRONMENTAL ADAPTATION — 26

CHAPTER FOUR
HUMAN AND SOCIAL ADAPTATION — 33

CHAPTER FIVE
GLOBAL SCALE ADAPTATION — 40

CHAPTER SIX
MULTI-LEVEL ADAPTATION — 46

CONCLUSION
ADAPTATION FOR FUTURE GENERATIONS — 54

Glossary — 56
Source Notes — 58
Selected Bibliography — 59
Further Information — 60
Index — 62

INTRODUCTION

Floods can destroy homes, make towns disappear, and put lives in danger. Southern California experienced destructive floods in the winter between 2022 and 2023. These floods caused blackouts at more than two hundred thousand homes and resulted in at least eighteen deaths.

Climate change makes floods more common and more powerful. Rising sea levels mean coastlines experience this the most. From 1970 to 2020, the chance of experiencing a flood along the US coastline increased by more than 900 percent, threatening public safety in coastal towns. This is why Burlingame and Millbrae, two small coastal cities in California, joined forces to help with climate change risks and flooding threats. With government funding and support, they designed a plan that protects 1.6 miles (2.6 km) of coastline from flooding for up to 6 feet (1.8 m) of sea level rise.

Their action of adjusting in response to the threat of floods is an example of adaptation. Adaptation is any act to change and become better suited to a new environment or situation. Both individuals and groups can adapt. Also, adaptations can be biological or behavioral. In biology, an adaptation is any trait that is passed down from a parent. For example, the Arctic fox has certain genes that give it a thick, white fur coat. Each winter, when temperatures begin to drop, the foxes' coats grow thicker and lose pigment. The pigment loss makes them whiter, improving their camouflage in snowy and icy landscapes, and the thicker fur helps keep in heat.

A behavioral adaptation is a learned behavior that helps plants and animals survive. For example, to survive the frigid Antarctic winters, emperor penguins form huddles. The huddles help retain and transfer heat between them. Going inside or resting in the shade to protect yourself from the sun on a hot day is also a behavioral adaptation. So is Burlingame and Millbrae's plan to protect coastlines from flooding.

Deep into the winter, the Arctic fox's coat is thick and white.

Adaptation is crucial to the survival of all organisms on Earth when conditions change. What happens when organisms do not adapt? What would happen if emperor penguins did not huddle, if Arctic foxes had thinner and darker fur coats, or if you did not escape the sun when you were overheating? Also, what would happen if these adaptations did not occur quickly enough? This is when the risk of extinction arises and threatens life on Earth.

Just like all other major changes in climate throughout history, some species will effortlessly adapt to the impacts of climate change, while others may vanish. Take the golden toad, for example, a species that went extinct in 1989. Some scientists believe the rising temperatures caused by climate change are to blame.

Climate Change

To better understand why and how life on Earth is adapting—or will adapt—to climate change, it helps to understand exactly what climate change is. Climate change is the long-term shift in global climates, temperatures, seasons, and weather patterns. It is happening faster than ever because of human activity.

Humans burn fossil fuels such as coal and gas to get power and energy. Burning these materials gives off fossil fuel emissions. The emissions gather in the atmosphere and form a layer that acts like the walls of a greenhouse, allowing sunlight to enter and trapping it. This is called the greenhouse gas effect. It leads to global warming—the rising of Earth's average temperatures.

Global warming is a big part of climate change. Other effects include melting sea ice and sea level rise, more

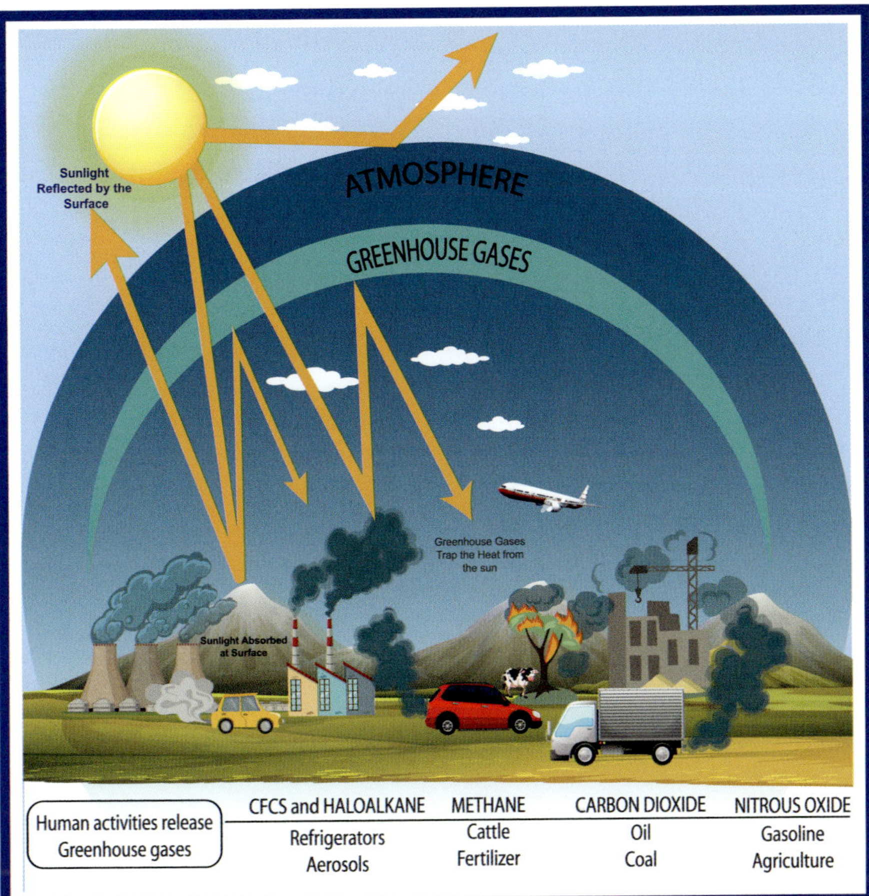

This illustration of how the greenhouse effect works shows that human-made gases trap a lot of heat in the atmosphere.

frequent and more intense droughts, floods, heat waves, and wildfires, as well as other types of intense weather and natural disasters.

Climate change is a global crisis that threatens extinction for some species and the quality of life for all. By 2027 scientists predict that global temperature averages could reach up to 3.24°F (1.8°C) above the average from the late nineteenth century. This few degrees' difference could have deadly consequences, causing catastrophic weather events and bringing about unpredictable change. Even if countries and communities stop greenhouse gas emissions altogether, some impacts of climate change will persist because of the change that has already occurred. So, more than ever, climate change adaptation is required at all scales, from global organizations to individuals.

This book will explain all the parts of climate change adaptation. It will cover how scientists measure adaptation, and outline adaptations that are already in place or possible to help humanity adjust to our changing climate.

CHAPTER ONE
Measuring Adaptation

Climate change research has evolved a lot since scientists began to investigate rising temperatures. Eunice Newton Foote, who studied water vapor and how the water in Earth's air controls global temperatures, first discovered the greenhouse effect in the 1850s. Late in that decade John Tyndall built on Foote's observations and was the first to measure radiation absorption by different gases in our atmosphere. In 1896 scientist Svante Arrhenius announced his prediction that changes in the amounts of carbon dioxide and other gases in our atmosphere would change our climate. After Arrhenius' prediction, evidence continued to pile up. About forty years later, another scientist, Guy Callender, used physics equations and global weather stations to link the extra (human-emitted) CO_2 in our atmosphere to rising global temperatures.

As climate change became better understood, scientists continued to unravel the greenhouse gas effect and uncover Earth's ancient climates. Then in the 1950s, researchers developed climate models based on Callender's equations,

The greenhouse effect is named for the atmosphere acting like an actual greenhouse, which traps heat to help control growing conditions for plants.

which helped them better understand what climate change could look like in the future. Climate models are computer programs that are comparable to simulations. They use equations based on Earth's natural processes to predict possible future scenarios of climate change.

These advancements equipped scientists with the knowledge needed to prepare for, take advantage of, and adapt to climate change's impacts. Modern climate scientists still monitor greenhouse gas emissions and other physical factors in climate change. But climate change scientists, research groups, and organizations around the globe now also focus on studying social components of climate change, such as adaptation.

The Intergovernmental Panel on Climate Change (IPCC), a United Nations (UN) group that focuses on climate science, defines climate change adaptation as an adjustment in social, ecological, or environmental contexts in response to current or future expected climate change impacts. It is relatively easy to study chemicals, measure temperatures, and analyze weather patterns. It is a much different challenge to make sense of abstract concepts such as adaptation. So, how do people study the social features of climate change?

Measuring Adaptation

Although it's harder, climate change scientists can study and measure adaptation just like they study and measure weather and temperature increases. They can figure out how likely someone is to adapt to climate change or how vulnerable they are to its consequences. They do so by using special adaptation measuring techniques for both environments and people. To understand these techniques, the first step is to understand what scientists are measuring.

There are several different terms used in climate change adaptation science. These terms are based on measurable factors and can be divided into three categories. There are:

1. terms describing the risks of climate change
2. terms related to how groups and individuals respond to climate change
3. terms that describe the health and strength of the group or individual

Measuring adaptation is important for developing climate adaptation plans. These plans consist of actions that improve adaptation and reduce harmful impacts of climate change.

Risk, Hazards, and Exposure

Three of the most important terms describing the severity and different types of threats of climate change are *risk*, *hazards*, and *exposure*. As the IPCC states, risk can be thought of as the "potential for adverse [negative] consequences for humans or ecological systems." Scientists measure risk based on climate hazards and climate exposure. A hazard is a threat that can cause damage. Exposure is how much humans and the environment face hazards and changes in climate. Let's look at a real-life example to get a better idea of how these terms affect the threat of climate change.

Imagine that you would like to compare the risk, hazards, and exposure of two different communities. One is

Coastal states such as South Carolina commonly face flooding after storms. In 2024 Hurricane Helene brought widespread flooding to cities such as Greenville.

a coastal community that faces flood threats and disappearing coastlines. The other community is located one hour's drive inland, and its biggest climate change concern is warmer temperatures. In this case, the coastal community is more at risk than the inland one because it is more exposed to climate change hazards (flooding and rising sea levels) due to its location.

Mitigation vs. Adaptation

Mitigation and adaptation are all about people's responses to climate change threats. While adaptation is adjusting to the impacts of climate change, mitigation is the actions and adjustments made to limit human activity that causes climate change and to reduce future impacts. For example, if you were to carpool, use less electricity, or participate in fossil fuel-banning campaigns, you would be taking action to reduce climate change. These actions would be climate change mitigation. But if people in your town were to start tinting their windows, purchasing solar panels, painting their houses white, and taking other actions to deal with rising temperatures and greater sun exposure, they would be adjusting to climate change. They would be participating in adaptation.

Resilience, Adaptive Capacity, and Vulnerability

The terms that describe the overall state, health, and strength of groups or individuals are *resilience*, *adaptive capacity*, and *vulnerability*. Resilience is the amount of climate change

Polar bears are one of many species that are especially vulnerable to climate change impacts.

that a group, individual, or environment can handle while maintaining their structure and function. Adaptive capacity is the ability that a group or individual has to adapt to negative climate change impacts. Vulnerability is how much a social group or the environment is unable to cope with those impacts.

Resilience, adaptive capacity, and vulnerability are some of the most studied concepts in climate change adaptation science. Figuring out how to assess and measure vulnerability is crucial to knowing who needs the most help to adapt to climate change. Studying resilience and adaptive capacity is also key since this allows scientists to learn who adapts to climate change most efficiently. From there, scientists can determine successful adaptation strategies that can be applied in other vulnerable communities. In other words, defining and measuring these three concepts is crucial to identifying vulnerable groups and carrying out more effective adaptation strategies around the world.

Another important concept is *sensitivity*. Sensitivity is how likely it is that a person, community, or area is going to be impacted by an event. The impact can be positive or negative. If there is a high chance of being impacted, the sensitivity will be high, too. When measuring sensitivity to climate change, scientists usually measure how likely people or areas are to be impacted by climate-related events such as flooding or temperature changes.

Finding a Formula

Measuring vulnerability or exposure relies on indicators. Indicators are factors that influence vulnerability, adaptive capacity, or resilience. For example, if you are measuring the adaptive capacity of different countries, you might look for indicators relating to government support, human resources, or wealth. Some of those indicators might include the country's education statistics, employment rates, worker benefits and wages, available disaster support, available emergency plans, and more. Surveys are also a great tool for measuring vulnerability. Let's look at a real-life example to see how scientists measure vulnerability between different groups.

The Productive Safety Net Program

Ethiopia struggles with poverty, food security, and poor infrastructure. These issues have become even more challenging due to severe climate change impacts and droughts. They do not have enough resources to fight these impacts. To help improve the resilience of its citizens, the Ethiopian government launched the Productive Safety Net Program (PSNP) in 2005. The PSNP uses tools such as statistical data and surveys to find the most vulnerable citizens. Then the group provides them with food and funds in times of climate change-caused droughts, floods, and delayed rains. Some of the most notable positive outcomes of the PSNP are increased crop yields, improved family welfare, and even improved cognitive development of the children of the identified families, which results from access to more nutritious food. PSNP and its outcomes are just one example of the importance of studying and measuring concepts such as vulnerability.

Less than 15 percent of Ethiopians had access to clean water in 2024. When countries already face challenges such as this one, it makes it harder to fund climate change adaptation.

A group of scientists in Cape Town, South Africa, set out to measure the vulnerability of coastal communities to the impacts of climate change. They aimed to better understand and help improve the adaptive capacity of these communities. First the scientists designed surveys that asked questions about the exposure, adaptive capacity, and sensitivity of the communities. Some questions asked the participants to rate the severity of recent storms (exposure). Others asked about the state of their homes, town buildings, and other infrastructure (sensitivity). Finally the survey asked about emergency plans and savings (adaptive capacity). The scientists assigned numbers to each question, with 1 being very vulnerable and 4 being not vulnerable. In the end, each participant got an average score representing their sensitivity, exposure, and adaptive capacity. From there, the scientists calculated a single vulnerability score for each individual and then each community by using this formula:

vulnerability = exposure + sensitivity - adaptive capacity

In short, the scientists identified adaptation factors, then used indicators and surveys to measure the vulnerability of the coastal communities of South Africa. By sharing their findings with policymakers and working with local stakeholders, they were able to better understand what people needed to cope with climate change. For example, some communities needed better infrastructure that could handle more frequent storms. Others needed more job opportunities because climate change threatened their current jobs.

Hundreds of tetrapods sit piled against a seawall in Cape Town. The concrete block structures are designed to minimize the effects of waves.

The results of studies such as this one help governments and organizations decide what actions to take to help people adapt. But for these studies to be worthwhile, these groups must actually take those actions. Sometimes this is where the challenges of climate change adaptation reside.

CHAPTER TWO

Challenges of Adaptation

The negative impacts of climate change are quickly getting worse and more common. This makes adaptation more complex, more expensive, and harder to figure out. As people are faced with more and more severe weather pattern changes, they must improvise, often taking actions that neither they nor their ancestors have ever taken before. In addition to the unfamiliarity with climate change and adaptation itself, there are four primary reasons why climate change adaptation is so difficult. These include a lack of financial resources, institutional or governmental barriers, a lack of knowledge or information, and even the pesky challenge of maladaptation.

Lack of Financial Resources

Climate change adaptation requires planning, resources, and investment. For example, let's look at city planning for areas that struggle with climate change-caused flooding. Flood risk planning can be as simple as individuals putting flood drains in and around their homes and using waterproofing paint to seal gaps or openings in walls, especially in their basements. It can also be as complicated as restructuring entire towns. This might include building diversion canals, which carry flood water away from the town, and flood barriers. Some adaptation plans for flood risk prevention even suggest rebuilding city buildings, power sources, roads, and other transportation routes. These rebuilds might also include raising buildings above future expected sea levels or building sea walls or similar barriers along the coast for extra protection. No matter the actions required, they need funding. And they can be very costly. A study conducted by the United States Climate Disclosure Project

The floodgate along the San Antonio River in Texas is used to divert rising water from heavy rains.

estimated that the average flood risk plan alone costs over $300 million, up to three-quarters of which is covered by the federal government.

The United Nations predicts that by 2050 some countries will need to spend around $500 billion each year on climate change adaptation. Even the wealthiest countries might not have the financial resources to fund these plans. What is more, the countries that most lack the financial resources to adapt to climate change are the most affected and the most in need of funds and resources. This leads to the next challenge: government limitations.

Government Limitations and Lack of Knowledge

In addition to the lack of funds, some governments might not have the capacity to organize climate change adaptation measures. In many cases, other global crises compete for funds and resources. For example, in countries where food security is lacking and poverty is high, available funds might go toward building infrastructure for food sources, such as storage facilities, farms, processing centers, and packaging centers, instead of building dams and canals for flood risk prevention. Another governmental barrier to successful climate change adaptation is a lack of communication. Governments that lack effective leadership and are not directly in touch with regions and communities have poor communication. This results in strong, effective policies and plans going to waste because of an avoidable disconnect. For example, if a government sets up a policy limiting fossil fuel use but they do not communicate it to the public or

In West Africa, where drought due to climate change has decimated the food supply in many countries, adaptation funding may be used to build infrastructure to support food production and storage.

directly designate anyone to enforce the policy, the efforts and resources used to create the policy go to waste because no one is following it.

In some cases, there can also be a knowledge gap in government, resulting in unclear directions on how to adapt. For example, some governments might not have a team of scientists to assess or study climate change and adaptation. Without proper assessments or accurate information, it is hard to know where to invest and how to make sound decisions. This lack of clarity can result in no adaptation action plans being created or implemented or in plans with little enforcement or efficiency. As we discussed, climate change affects everyone and everywhere differently. This means that every adaptation plan is unique and requires locally relevant information and studies. An adaptation plan that is put together quickly, without taking into account the exact vulnerabilities of a community or region, will likely be ineffective or lead to an even bigger problem—maladaptation.

Maladaptation

Have you ever tried to solve a problem only to make it worse? Perhaps you got a cut and covered it with a bandage, only to realize that the bandage did not allow the cut to heal and caused an infection instead. The bandage would be an example of day-to-day maladaptation—a would-be solution to a problem that backfired and made the problem worse.

An example of climate change maladaptation could be planting trees to help absorb carbon out of the atmosphere. While this is a great solution in some areas, it is not in others. For example, if the area is dealing with drought and heat waves, the extra trees will make it easier for fire to start and spread. So, in this case, the carbon-absorbing trees are a fire hazard, worsening the threat of wildfire. Individuals might also have a day-to-day maladaptation to climate change. For example, someone might adapt to heat waves or longer winters by amping up their air conditioning or heaters. But this temporary fix contributes to the carbon dioxide emissions that cause climate change and worsen the heat waves and frigid winters they are trying to avoid.

Investments, Techno-solutions, and Maladaptation

The global cost of climate change disasters is expected to reach $3 trillion a year by 2050. In response to the massive costs, the United Nations Framework Convention on Climate Change (UNFCCC) created the International Adaptation Fund in 2001 to help the lowest-income and most vulnerable countries adapt to climate change. This organization pools financial resources to fund adaptation in these countries. The Adaptation Fund, which we'll discuss more in chapter five, is putting big money toward climate change adaptation efforts. But some experts think that this funding might lead to maladaptation. This can be true, especially if most of the funding goes toward large technology-based solutions, some of which are more expensive and less effective than nature-based solutions. Some climate scientists believe that investments in these techno-solutions lead to a false sense of security and become another form of maladaptation. One example of this is carbon capture and storage facilities, which are often expensive and had a 90 percent failure rate between 2000 and the 2020s. There are several facilities where CO_2 has been trapped underground that are now abandoned and could end up releasing it back into the atmosphere. Alternatively, nature-based solutions, such as reducing destruction to ecosystems that naturally and successfully capture carbon, are much cheaper and more successful in the long term.

Carbon capture and storage facilities catch carbon dioxide emissions and store them away. They help reduce emissions in theory but have a poor record of success.

Those were smaller examples. When maladaptation happens on a larger scale, such as when entire governments make uninformed decisions, the consequences can be disastrous. Climate change maladaptation can create new problems and worsen others and their consequences for neighboring groups. For example, coastal erosion and sea level rise threaten the islands of Fiji. To mitigate these risks, some communities built seawalls. But the walls made flooding worse in nearby areas and contributed to more coastal erosion in neighboring communities. In addition to struggling with the cost and damage of the initial flooding, those other Fiji communities are also paying for the consequences of their neighbors' maladaptive solutions.

So, when faced with financial restraints, governmental limitations, knowledge gaps, and the impacts of maladaptation, how can we adapt to climate change? The solutions are different for the environment and humanity.

CHAPTER THREE

Environmental Adaptation

One of the reasons climate change is so harmful to the environment is because it affects biodiversity in every ecosystem and habitat, destroying key elements of the natural world and raising the risk of extinction. Biodiversity is the amount and variety of plant and animal species that are found in an ecosystem, from the microscopic bacteria to the apex predators that sit at the top of the food chain. Biodiversity includes all the varieties and makeup of life on Earth and is crucial to humanity's survival. Thanks to the biodiversity of our planet, we have clean air to breathe, clean water to drink, food to eat, and an environment that ensures our health and quality of life.

What is more, biodiversity helps in the fight against climate change. Some habitats, such as terrestrial (land-based), mangrove, and kelp forests, have a unique ability to absorb carbon from our atmosphere, reducing greenhouse gases and the impacts of climate change. But human activities such as deforestation and climate change impacts such as storms, droughts, floods, and other natural disasters are destroying these habitats. As they are destroyed, these carbon-absorbing environments release excess carbon back into the atmosphere and contribute to climate change.

Since climate affects animal behavior, plant growth, species health, and all biological processes, even small climate shifts can trigger big changes and transform entire ecosystems. For example, if one species' population declines, migrates to a different ecosystem, or goes extinct, these shifts will have a chain reaction. The absence of the species will affect the original habitat's entire food chain and cycles, changing life for all species of the ecosystem. So, how do wildlife and our planet's ecosystems adapt to a changing climate?

Adaptation for Different Species

Many species will successfully adapt to and even benefit from climate change. Others will fail to adapt mainly because of the severity and pace of climate change. Climate models predict that if humanity does not address greenhouse gas emissions,

Climate change threatens Adélie penguins in Antarctica because melting ice reduces the availability of tiny fish called krill, which are critical for the penguins' survival.

global average temperatures could reach up to 8°F (4.5°C) above pre-Industrial Revolution (1733–1913) averages by 2100. This could put more than half of the plant and animal species on the planet on the brink of extinction. We could also lose most of the planet's biodiversity. This would leave animals, plants, and insects no choice but to adapt at record speed. Already, some species are changing their migration patterns, changing their diets, moving to cooler climates, and even adjusting their breeding cycles.

Some animals have specific physical features designed to handle extreme temperatures. Others develop different behaviors to cope with extreme temperatures. So, as temperatures change, animals will have to adapt either physically or behaviorally—or both. For example, some birds are adapting to warmer temperatures by developing larger bills, or beaks. In hotter and more tropical environments, birds have large bills since bills help to get rid of heat, lowering body temperature. Scientists who study birds have noted a slow increase in bill size in many bird species, such as the Australian parrot, where temperatures are rising. Similarly, animals such as wood mice are developing longer tails and longer limbs, which are body parts that also help dissipate heat. As for behavioral adaptations, over two hundred bird species have changed their nesting sites to cooler habitats (those that are nearer the poles and at higher elevations) since the early 1900s.

On the other hand, some species have not adapted very well. Ectotherms are cold-blooded animals, including most reptiles, amphibians, and insects, that do not control their body temperature internally. They depend on the heat from the sun and Earth's surface to stay warm and water, shade, or other chillier areas to cool down. So, as temperatures rise,

The Australian parrot has begun adapting to climate change with an increase in beak size over each generation. Birds lose heat most easily through their beaks.

they will need to either move to higher elevations where temperatures are lower, expand their range to other cooler areas, spend more time in the shade, or adapt their bodies to tolerate more heat. But many ectotherms don't seem to be doing that. For example, scientists have monitored lizard populations in Mexico since the 1970s. They found that as temperatures increased, local lizard populations were going extinct, and the overall biodiversity of lizards was greatly reduced. The scientists noted that many of these populations were heat sensitive and that more than half of all lizard populations could go extinct by 2080 if greenhouse gases are not reduced, and climate change persists.

Adaptations in Different Habitats

Almost every habitat on Earth is changing, causing every species to change and adapt as well. Oceans, forests, and deserts struggle with different challenges. Just as some species will adapt while others face extinction, some habitats will thrive while others perish. Also, like some individual species, some habitats faced with the threat of climate change have already developed specific adaptations.

Climate change greatly impacts ocean habitats. As more greenhouse gases are emitted and temperatures rise, the ocean acts as a sponge. It absorbs excess heat and carbon dioxide. This makes the water warmer and more acidic, which causes glacial melting, sea level rise, ocean heat waves, low oxygen levels, coral bleaching, and changes in ocean currents. To adapt to these impacts, marine creatures are changing their distribution, which is sort of like moving to a new address. Marine biologists have found that ocean species are moving to cooler waters with better oxygen levels and more comfortable temperatures.

Warming oceans threaten species such as North Atlantic right whales, which are moving toward the North Pole to find cooler waters. It is believed that fewer than five hundred of these whales still exist.

Indigenous Solutions To Adaptation

The UNFCCC highlights Indigenous practices as some of the best climate change adaptations. For example, Indigenous communities in Nepal, such as the Chepang and Tharu peoples, are adapting by planting native, community-managed forests. These forests are helping the environment through carbon capture. At the same time, the forests promote cultural preservation by incorporating ancient traditions, community engagement, and forest stewardship. The UNFCCC is facilitating similar "village common forests" in Kamalchhori, Bangladesh, for the positive environmental impacts and to help villages meet their daily needs. These forests help protect biodiversity and aid adaptation of Indigenous communities such as the Chakma and Marma peoples, as well as providing more food, water, and medicinal resources. The secretary of the Kamalchhori community cooperation states, "The state of our village common forest has changed magically as the dependency on the forest has reduced drastically."

Planting new trees in the community-managed forest has helped the environment in Nepal but has also promoted cultural preservation for the Tharu people.

Some of the biggest climate change threats to forest habitats include heat waves, forest fires, disease, insect invasions, and increases in non-native species. Tropical forests, mangroves, and agricultural forests will all be affected differently and require different adaptations. Many people have stepped in to protect these habitats and help them adapt based on what they need. For example, forest managers use controlled burning in areas where forest fires are a threat. This gets rid of dry, dead vegetation that burns easily, helping prevent the start and spread of forest fires. In many types of forests, managers also plant a variety of tree species to increase the biodiversity of the ecosystem. This also reduces climate change impacts since trees capture and store carbon from our atmosphere.

As climate change and global warming persist, deserts are warming up and expanding. They are gradually becoming some of the most vulnerable habitats on Earth. Desert species already faced reduced water access and potential heat stress. These conditions are getting worse. In addition, many desert species are ectotherms, making them some of the most vulnerable species to climate change. To help desert ecosystems adapt, land managers are planting vegetation to increase biodiversity. This helps because higher biodiversity reduces the risk of diseases, improves the resilience of the ecosystem, and decreases the risk of extinction. They are also implementing strategies to improve soil quality and conserve water.

In addition to the value of conserving nature for nature's sake, there are more reasons why humanity should help protect all habitats against climate change. We are financially, socially, and physically dependent on these ecosystems. The survival of all species and our future relies on the environment's ability to adapt.

CHAPTER FOUR
Human and Social Adaptation

Now we have an idea of how climate change affects different habitats and some ways they can adapt to its impacts. But what does adaptation look like for humanity? Every individual, community, culture, and country will demand unique adaptation plans. In general, there are three types of adaptation actions that people can take (incremental, transformational, and proactive or anticipatory) and four different adaptation approaches (institutional, infrastructural, behavioral, and nature-based) when it comes to climate change.

Human Adaptation Actions

Incremental adaptation plans consist of small actions taken over a long period. One example of incremental adaptation is when farmers switch to more resilient crop species. Farmers can also change the timing of when they plant and harvest crops. Other examples include when coastal communities improve beach conditions and when forestry managers adapt by adding nutrients to improve soil quality, which helps both plant and animal health. These changes contribute bit by bit to improving the land's adaptive capacity.

With the high rate of climate change, some systems need more drastic measures than incremental adaptation. This is where transformational adaptation plans come in handy. Transformational adaptation is based on big, dramatic changes. In extreme cases, some communities are relocating to entirely new places. For example, in 2014 the island village of Vendiola in Fiji had to relocate because of rising sea levels. Likewise, in Shishmaref, Alaska, coastlines are melting and disappearing into the sea. So, villagers voted in 2016 to relocate and move inland. While not always this extreme, transformational adaptation plans are still life-changing for everyone involved.

Farmers changing when they plant and harvest their crops is an example of incremental adaptation.

Proactive or anticipatory adaptation is when individuals or groups take action before they observe any climate change impacts. This form of adaptation can be either incremental or transformational. In either case, scientists help predict what impacts people will face. Laws focusing on proactive adaptation are based on studies instead of sudden events. Through this type of adaptation, there is even the opportunity to not only predict climate change events but also take advantage of them. For example, in some high-altitude areas, climate change has caused seasons to shift, bringing earlier springs. This makes the soil and land more fertile earlier in the year. Farmers can have a longer growing season and produce more crops if they are prepared to plant earlier.

Human Adaptation Approaches

The differences between the three adaptation actions reside in their timing and the size of the actions they call for. But the four approaches differ based on the methods used and who is making the decisions.

Institutional adaptation approaches are used by or in economies, policymakers, laws, regulations, and government programs. An example of institutional adaptation is Columbia's country-wide green building code. The South American country introduced the code in 2015, setting more sustainable standards for water, energy, and material use for their buildings. Another example is British Columbia's carbon tax policy. The Canadian province enacted the policy to help reduce emissions by demanding fees for fossil fuel use. For instance, the tax is collected from individuals at gas pumps. The tax is also

Canadians in British Columbia pay more at the pump due to a carbon tax premium charged for using fossil fuels.

charged to large-scale businesses based on their transportation, electricity, and fossil fuel-backed activities.

Infrastructural adaptations focus on buildings, high-tech solutions, and innovative architecture. Some innovative technologies include renewable energy sources such as solar panels, hydropower dams, and wind turbine farms. Other technologies include those that help recycle resources and use them more sustainably. For instance, smart bins are trash cans controlled by artificial intelligence that help sort garbage, detect recyclable waste, and reduce landfill waste. Additionally, some technologies help reduce our greenhouse gas emissions and help us lead more sustainable lives. These include electric cars to reduce fossil-fueled transportation, the exploration of hydrogen as opposed to coal for fuel to reduce carbon emissions, and carbon capture inventions to remove

A Guide To Climate-Resilient Building

The United Nations Environment Programme (UNEP) has created practical guides for constructing climate-resilient buildings. Their guides provide suggestions and solutions for responding to, adapting to, and preventing climate change-caused risks. For example, in locations struggling with heat waves, UNEP offers suggestions to help buildings reduce trapped indoor heat. One suggestion is to plant tall, local tree species to help shade homes and block the sun while allowing breezes to pass through. In areas prone to cyclones and increasing winds, they provide tips for roof and building shapes that are more wind-resistant. In areas that are at risk of flooding, they outline stilted and elevated structures and suggest water-resilient materials for building. They also provide a checklist of considerations that should be standard for new building projects in certain areas since building plans depend on local conditions. They always suggest researching local laws and building codes, incorporating local wisdom and modern science, and considering nature-based solutions to climate change impacts.

In areas that often experience flooding, the UNEP recommends elevating houses above possible floodwater levels.

carbon from the atmosphere. Other modern technologies, including satellites, can also help us better monitor climate change and greenhouse gas emissions.

Behavioral adaptations revolve around cultural practices, household habits, social norms, and community approaches. These adaptations involve day-to-day behaviors, such as decreasing water and electricity usage. Other behavioral adaptations include agricultural practices such as planting a greater diversity of crops, transportation adaptations such as carpooling or taking the bus, and any other habits or practices that people change to reduce humanity's overall carbon footprint. Individuals often make behavioral adaptations on their own. But these changes are even more powerful when they become norms that everyone follows.

Nature-based adaptations use the surrounding ecosystem to help adapt. Improving habitats by taking advantage of forests, streams, rivers, and other environments that store excess water is one nature-based solution. The groundwater of these environments provides clean drinking water in times of drought. People are planting more fire-resistant trees in fire-prone areas to decrease the spread of wildfires while increasing biodiversity. Improving the state of all types of forests and other coastal ecosystems helps reduce damage from big waves, sea level rise, and powerful storms such as hurricanes and cyclones. Great Green Wall Africa is a nature-based adaptation that the African Union began in response to drought and desertification in the Sahara Desert. Thousands of workers replanted native shrubs to prevent sandstorms. In some mountainous areas, people plant trees to prevent soil erosion. Erosion causes the ground and soil to become unstable, ultimately causing landslides. Planting trees helps

Replanting forests to prevent soil erosion is one of many nature-based adaptation solutions.

to bind the soil and prevent climate change-caused erosion and landslides. People are also planting more trees in cities susceptible to heat waves because of trees' ability to cool their surrounding environments. In fact, one tree can cool the surrounding environment more effectively than an air conditioner while also clearing out air pollution. While the extent of this cooling effect from any one tree or group of trees is difficult to measure, the local air temperature can be lowered by up to 10°F (5.6°C).

CHAPTER FIVE

Global Scale Adaptation

Climate change demands that we adapt on all scales: individually, as a community, as a country, and as a planet. This includes government at all levels, even including the homeowners associations in certain neighborhoods! Let's start with an overview of who is leading global climate change adaptation efforts.

Global Organizations

The United Nations is a political forum that addresses global issues such as climate change. To address climate change, the UN created the International Panel on Climate Change and the United Nations Framework Convention on Climate Change. They created the IPCC to provide reliable, globally relevant climate change science and solutions. Most of their adaptation studies revolve around reducing greenhouse gas emissions and developing plans to provide clean energy, improve air quality, and reduce vulnerability. The IPCC's Sixth Assessment Report in 2023 highlighted climate-resilient development as a key solution for adapting to and preventing climate change. This includes buildings and other infrastructure that operate with less fossil fuels and can withstand climate change impacts.

The IPCC's science is the backbone of the UNFCCC, the world's highest decision-making group for climate change adaptation. The UN created UNFCCC in 1992, and it is like a membership club that nearly all countries (195 out of 201 with full or partial international recognition) belong to. Every year the UNFCCC hosts a Conference of Parties (COP), where all members gather. There they make decisions about key climate actions, establish and divide responsibilities, divide adaptation funds, approve climate policies and laws, and explore solutions for climate change. One of the most notable global agreements they made is the 2021 Glasgow Climate Pact. The pact was the first climate agreement that explicitly requested that countries reduce emissions. It aims to reduce emissions by 45 percent from 2010 levels by 2030 and double funds toward adaptation efforts.

The International Adaptation Fund was formed in 2001 to help the lowest-income and most vulnerable countries adapt to climate change. This organization pools financial resources to fund adaptation in such communities. The lowest-income countries struggle most with climate change consequences and adaptation but contribute the least to greenhouse gas emissions. For example, researchers found that countries with lower incomes and weaker economies only contribute 10 percent of greenhouse gas emissions compared to industrialized nations with higher qualities of life and stronger economic growth. Yet the lower-income countries will endure more deaths, economic losses, and

Climate Action Network

One way that non-governmental organizations get involved in climate action is by supporting the Climate Action Network (CAN). CAN is the largest environmental network of companies, businesses, and conservation organizations that team up to specifically focus on the fight against climate change. With over 1,800 members in 130 countries, CAN works to put an end to fossil fuel use, hold governments accountable to meet climate targets, and take action to build a more sustainable future. As an individual, you can also get involved and support CAN by subscribing to their newsletter, donating to them, spreading awareness about their work and climate change, and keeping an eye out for early career internships.

Ending fossil fuel use is one of the primary goals of the Climate Action Network.

extreme weather events due to climate change. Plus, a 2020 study by a World Bank research group found that at least one hundred million people will be pushed further into poverty by 2030, making it even harder for their communities to fund climate change adaptations. The World Bank stated that these nations need external help, especially since "climate change is hindering poverty reduction and is a major threat going forward."

Over the years, the International Adaptation Fund has raised over $1 billion from governments and private donors. As an example of how some of the money is spent, the fund donated just under $7 million to southern Egypt between 2013 and 2020. They aimed to improve the region's adaptive capacity. To do so, the country used the money to install water-saving and climate-monitoring technologies. They also used the money to help locals develop new career skills and find more reliable jobs, ultimately reducing the poverty that prevents funding adaptation. They granted almost forty thousand loans to individuals and businesses to support women's empowerment, too. In addition, they improved agriculture by bringing in more resilient crops and improving soil fertility with more efficient irrigation techniques. These actions made the farmland 25 percent more fertile. Farmers reported that they lost 60 percent less crops during extreme weather events. Plus, these actions contributed to a 40 percent increase in citizens' yearly income. Income increases and the resulting reduction in poverty give citizens more resources and capacity to adapt to changes such as climate change impacts.

The International Adaptation Fund also analyzes the effectiveness of the adaptation plans that they fund. Based on

The International Adaptation Fund provided money to help farmers in southern Egypt bring in more resilient crops and improve soil fertility.

their studies, they come up with adaptation best practices and standards to improve adaptation all around the world.

Adaptation Plans in the United States

National organizations and agencies have also taken steps to help communities adapt to climate change. For example, the US Environmental Protection Agency (EPA) is a federal agency that aims to protect the environment and human health. One of the agency's methods to do this is by employing adaptation plans. They support plans from the national level down to state and local efforts, such as the Missouri Water Utility Climate Adaptation plan. Using the EPA's Climate Resilience Evaluation and Awareness Tool (CREAT), the community of Fredericktown, Missouri, identified and formed an adaptation plan to combat their biggest climate change threat: drought and water scarcity. They used CREAT to identify sources of drought, develop alternative water sources, and prepare for drought and climate change in the future.

Fredericktown is an example of how adaptation plans can succeed with adequate resources, direction, and government communication. As we discussed, failure to communicate can mean a perfectly tailored adaptation plan might go to waste. In this light, one important part of any adaptation plan, especially national ones, is the vertical integration plan. This is where nations, sub-authorities, local organizations, and individuals are linked to communicate, plan, share information, and craft more efficient adaptation plans. This way, everyone knows what the plan is and how to contribute to it.

Severe drought conditions in 2012 dried up lakes across Missouri and prompted the development of the Missouri Water Utility Climate Adaptation plan.

CHAPTER SIX

Multi-Level Adaptation

The UN, IPCC, COP events, and adaptation plans are the global backbone of climate change adaptation. But they are meaningless unless there is solid communication that links these global organizations to local communities. Their efforts are also only effective if they are combined with individual action. Think about it like this: Imagine that your school system wanted to become more environmentally friendly by reducing plastic use, encouraging more recycling, and teaching students about renewable energy and climate change. If education experts and those in charge of the school system made perfect execution plans without informing principals, teachers, and students, how effective would their efforts would be? In this same scenario, imagine that there were perfect plans and solid communication, but no individuals were taking action. All efforts in both cases would be wasted. Everyone must be involved in, or at least informed of, the process of creating and enacting solutions.

Community Adaptation

How you and your community adapt largely depends on the region you live in and which climate change impacts affect you. From drought and higher temperatures to floods and other extreme events, there are a variety of impacts you might face. The first step in community adaptation is to identify these risks, exposures, and threats, as well as the most vulnerable places or people. With this knowledge, communities can make adaptation plans, similar to how the Fredericktown community successfully created an adaptation plan for drought.

If your community is struggling with heat waves, do roads and bridges need to be rebuilt so they can withstand extreme heat? Government officials have suggested that investing in

If your community faces seasonal flooding, it should identify the risks of the flooding and make a plan to adapt and overcome them.

climate-resilient infrastructure is one of the wisest adaptation investments. For example, incorporating cool pavements into current and future cities helps communities reduce the impacts of heat waves. Cool pavements are made of water-based materials, which means they reflect heat instead of absorbing it. One city that has implemented cool pavements is Phoenix, Arizona. The city announced its cool pavement program in 2020. The first year was a success, cooling surfaces by up to 12°F (7°C) at peak sun hours. The positive outcomes led the city and communities to transform as much asphalt and concrete to cool surfaces as possible, with more than 120 miles (193 km) converted in 2023. If you and your community struggle with droughts and heatwaves, you can get in touch with legislators, write petitions, and educate others on cool pavements to take action to incorporate a cool pavement program into your city plans.

In addition to adding more climate-resilient infrastructure, Phoenix established the Cool Corridors Program, which is a plan to plant more trees and plants throughout the community. The plants help cool their surroundings. You and your community can also plant more trees for shade and cooling. The United States Department of Agriculture created a guide to tree species that are best for climate change prevention in different habitats. You can find the guide on their website.

If your community is situated near the coast, how will the impacts of flooding be prevented? Perhaps with walls, with structures that help break down waves, or by improving the infrastructure of homes. San Francisco, California, is facing major floods and coastline damage, with a more than 6-inch (15-cm) rise in sea level between 1950 and 2023. To combat this, San Francisco plans to spend over $5 billion to improve their city sea wall, which is their main solution to prevent damage from floods and storms. Smaller communities and neighborhoods can contribute to adaptation by installing stormwater pumps, improving stormwater management plans, and flood-proofing homes and other important buildings. For individuals, flood-proofing could include elevating their houses by either raising the bottom floor above flood levels or building an elevated floor within the house.

In mountainous communities, soil erosion is a common threat of climate change. So adaptation plans must address how landslides will be averted. In colder mountainous

San Francisco has one of the oldest seawalls in the country, with sections of it dating back more than a hundred years.

communities, extreme ice melts cause flooding and erosion. This is addressed by everything from modifying slope geometry to rerouting surface and underwater drainage. Methods vary based on the particular circumstances of each community. In contrast, the vulnerable mountainous communities in sunny Jamaica are grappling with climate change-caused hurricanes, erosion, and landslides. In the Jamaican hills, many people rely on coffee plantations and agriculture for food and job security, so climate change puts their livelihoods and way of life at risk. To combat these impacts, their adaptation plans include planting more trees. This is because trees help stabilize the soil and ground, preventing erosion. As an additional benefit, the planted trees help keep the climate misty and cool, which is ideal for coffee plants.

Adaptation for You

You can also take action individually around your home and in your community to help adapt to climate change. The actions that you take will depend on the kind of climate change impacts you are experiencing. For actions in and around your home, you can use resources provided by the EPA, including information about climate-resilient infrastructure, which tree species to plant, and more, to decide what will work best and is doable for you. Even simple actions such as clearing dead vegetation and weeds can help prevent climate change impacts and reduce the spread of wildfires.

In addition to researching resources, it is important to understand your home building plan and community

Race to Resilience

Do you want to take immediate action on climate change adaptation? Something you can do right now is register for Race to Resilience. Race to Resilience is an organization that aims to expand how many people are taking action to become more resilient against climate change. They want to reach four billion members by 2030. They offer the opportunity to create climate change adaptation initiatives that are relevant to you and your community. For example, they are supporting coral reef restoration efforts in Fiji, better weather information systems in East Africa, and nature-friendly sea walls to prevent storm damage in England.

Race to Resilience supports coral reef restoration projects in the South Pacific, such as this coral nursery that is growing coral to fill depleted reefs.

guidelines. A home building plan is the blueprint of your house. It includes sketches of each floor, information about whether your house is on a foundation, where pipes go, and more. Before planting trees around your property, it is wise to look over your home building plan to ensure that you and your family do not plant trees that would disrupt underground plumbing and other utilities.

If you want to create an impact that extends beyond your home, get involved in adaptation around your community. You can learn about the climate change impacts in your community and research solutions to these impacts. You can get involved with local organizations that are combating climate change near you or join or start a climate-focused club at school. You can also reach out to city planning groups and natural resource managers to learn more about what your community has planned for climate change adaptation.

It is important for you, your family or household, your neighbors, and even your school to consider how climate change will impact your community. You can help everyone around you think more about and prepare for climate change. Ask your caretakers about their insurance plans and climate change emergency plans. Find out if your household has insurance for extreme events such as flooding or storms. Encourage businesses to ditch fossil fuels and embrace renewable energy. Get involved at city council meetings. In fact, one of the most effective individual actions is getting involved in politics, no matter your age. Attending community, school board, or city council meetings is how you can have some of the most meaningful impacts. Learn about your legislators' adaptation plans and how they plan to handle your local risks. You can get in touch through letters

Unite with other climate conscious people in your community and start to make a difference.

or emails and by attending public events. When talking to your legislators, ask whether the structures and buildings in your town are prepared for predicted climate change events. Let your legislators know that you and your family support climate-smart policies.

As former vice president Al Gore famously stated, "Believe in the power of your own voice. The more noise you make, the more accountability you demand from your leaders, the more our world will change for the better."

CONCLUSION
Adaptation for Future Generations

Climate change is affecting our planet more and more each day, and adaptation is needed more than ever. Adaptation looks different for every country, habitat, community, species, culture, region, and human. While a bird might grow a larger bill to better handle the heat, a community might build more resilient homes to better handle storms. While some whales might change their annual migration patterns to find cooler seas, some coastal communities might migrate inland to avoid flooding and sea level rise. Climate change adaptation is so diverse that it can often feel overwhelming. This is why global organizations and climate scientists have found ways to measure climate change risks and vulnerability, making it easier to know which adaptations will be most needed and effective.

Adaptations can also seem difficult and too big for communities, countries, and the world to conquer. For example, some people get discouraged because rebuilding structures, relocating entire towns, and investing in climate change solutions is complex and expensive. However, there is something that is even more expensive than adaptation investments: climate change impacts. Protecting habitats and communities now means less damage and more lives saved in the future. According to the UN, investing $1.8 trillion in climate change adaptation efforts now could save $7.1 trillion in climate change damage repair later. Investing in adaptation saves time, money, and lives.

Governments, communities, and organizations recognize the undeniable value in adaptation. So while adaptation can be challenging, more and more groups are helping communities and habitats adapt—and succeeding, too. In 2023 alone, the EPA noted that more money was going into solar power than oil, California took five major oil companies to court to hold them accountable for environmental damage, Brazil halved the deforestation rates of the Amazon rainforest, and adaptation action plans are on the rise worldwide.

These examples are just a few of the many adaptation wins. There is nothing more important than investing in the protection of humanity and future generations. Therefore, there might be nothing more important than the actions you take to help our planet and humanity adapt to climate change.

You can also take part in climate action by attending protests, signing petitions, and more.

GLOSSARY

adaptation: the process of adjusting to change in a way that avoids harm or takes advantage of new opportunities

adaptive capacity: the potential for a system, habitat, group, or individual to adapt to changes, such as the impacts of climate change

biodiversity: the variability of nature, environments, ecosystems, and living organisms. Biodiversity is measured and compared between species, within species populations, and in entire ecosystems.

carbon dioxide (CO_2): a gas that is emitted upon burning fossil fuels such as oil, gas, and coal. CO_2 is a major contributor to global warming and climate change due to its potency, lifetime, and significant emissions.

carbon sequestration: a process of absorbing and storing carbon dioxide from our atmosphere, which kelp, plants, trees, and certain geological features do naturally

climate model: a computer program based on equations that represent Earth's climate and natural processes. Climate models are used to predict future climates based on different scenarios.

deforestation: the action of clearing a wide area of trees and natural habitat; the overall breaking down of forests and natural environments

desertification: the breaking down of land and reduction in soil fertility caused by global warming, storms, and the overall reduction of land

drought: a long period of abnormally dry conditions and less precipitation, leading to long-lasting effects on soil moisture

ecosystem: a biological community of living organisms and their interactions with each other and their specific environment

emission: the release of pollutants, gases, and chemicals into the atmosphere

exposure: in the context of climate change, the degree that a system, habitat, group, or individual experiences the presence of a climate change impact

food security: a situation where all humans have access to and can afford sufficient, safe, and nutritious food that meets all dietary needs

greenhouse gas: any of the gases that are emitted into the atmosphere and contribute to the greenhouse effect, which leads to global warming and climate change

heat wave: a period of two or more days of abnormally hot temperatures and excessive humidity

Industrial Revolution: the rapid societal transition from small-scale production and producing most goods by hand to mass production and a dependency on fossil fuels

mitigation: an action that is taken to prevent or reduce the likelihood of future harm or loss

renewable energy: energy that is derived from a source that replenishes itself naturally over time and doesn't run out, such as solar power

resilience: the capacity of environmental, human, or economic systems to cope with hazards, events, or harmful impacts of global change such as climate change

sensitivity: the degree to which climate change affects a system, habitat, group, or individual

sustainable: of, relating to, or being a method of harvesting or using a resource so that the resource is not depleted or permanently damaged

vulnerable: the state and predisposition to be adversely affected or the lack of ability to avoid a hazard

SOURCE NOTES

12 "Potential for adverse . . . or ecological systems." Margot Hurlbert and Jagdish Krishnaswamy, "Risk Management and Decision Making in Relation to Sustainable Development," IPCC Special Report on Climate Change and Land, accessed 11/27/24, https://www.ipcc.ch/srccl/chapter/chapter-7/.

31 "The state of . . . has reduced drastically": Abu Siddique, "In Bangladesh, a Community Comes Together to Save a Life-Giving Forest," Mongabay, May 19, 2022, https://news.mongabay.com/2022/05/in-bangladesh-a-community-comes-together-to-save-a-life-giving-forest/.

43 "Climate change is . . . threat going forward": Russell Taylor, "Sustainable Development Goals and the Impact of Global Conflict, Extreme Poverty and Climate-Related Emergencies," House of Lords Library, October 10, 2024, https://lordslibrary.parliament.uk/sustainable-development-goals-and-the-impact-of-global-conflict-extreme-poverty-and-climate-related-emergencies/.

53 "Believe in the . . . for the better": "Al Gore, Environmental Activist and U.S. Vice President, Born (1948)," Today in Conservation, March 31, 2019, https://todayinconservation.com/2019/03/march-31-al-gore-environmental-activist-and-u-s-vice-president-born-1948.

SELECTED BIBLIOGRAPHY

Adger, W. Neil, Nigel W. Arnell, and Emma L. Tompkins. "Successful Adaptation to Climate Change across Scales." *Global Environmental Change* 15, no. 2 (2005): 77–86. https://doi.org/10.1016/j.gloenvcha.2004.12.005.

Barnett, Jon, and Saffron O'Neill. "Maladaptation." *Global Environmental Change* 20, no. 2 (2010): 211–213.

Folke, Carl, Stephen R. Carpenter, Brian Walker, Marten Scheffer, Terry Chapin, and Johan Rockström. "Resilience Thinking: Integrating Resilience, Adaptability and Transformability." *Ecology and Society* 15, no. 4 (December 2010). http://www.jstor.org/stable/26268226.

Hoegh-Guldberg, Ove, Daniela Jacob, Michael Taylor, et al. "Impacts of 1.5°C Global Warming on Natural and Human Systems." In *Global Warming of 1.5°C. An IPCC Special Report on the impacts of global warming of 1.5°C above pre-industrial levels and related global greenhouse gas emission pathways, in the context of strengthening the global response to the threat of climate change, sustainable development, and efforts to eradicate poverty.* Edited by Masson-Delmotte, Valérie, Pan mao Zhai, et al., 175–311. Cambridge, UK: Cambridge University Press, 2022.

Jahan, Sam. "Third of Bangladesh Underwater as Monsoon Drenches Region." Phys.org, July 14, 2020. https://phys.org/news/2020-07-bangladesh-underwater-monsoon-drenches-region.html.

Joem, Birkmann, Emma Liwenga, Rajiv Pandey, et al. "Poverty, Livelihoods and Sustainable Development." In *Climate Change 2022: Impacts, Adaptation, and Vulnerability.* Edited by Pörtner Hans-O., Debra C. Roberts, Melinda Tignor, et al., 1171–1284. Cambridge, UK: Cambridge University Press, 2022.

FURTHER INFORMATION

BOOKS

Davenport, Leslie. *All the Feelings Under the Sun: How to Deal with Climate Change.* Washington, DC: Magination Press, 2021.
Get an expert understanding of the science behind the climate crisis. You can also engage with lots of self-guided activities, journaling prompts, and useful resources.

McPherson, Stephanie Sammartino. *Hothouse Earth: The Climate Crisis and the Importance of Carbon Neutrality.* Minneapolis: Twenty-First Century Books, 2021.
This book examines how science, politics, and social justice must all be part of the equation to counteract climate change.

Minoglio, Andrea. *Our World Out of Balance: Understanding Climate Change and What We Can Do.* San Francisco: Blue Dot Kids Press, 2021.
Find out more about how humans have thrown the planet off-balance and ways we can work together to be part of the solution and create a healthier world.

Prentice, Andy, and Eddie Reynolds. *Understanding Climate Change.* London: Usborne, 2024.
Explore complex questions such as: How does the climate work? What are we doing to change it? What can we do differently to avoid the worst outcomes? This book also suggests tips on setting realistic goals in the fight against climate change.

Thomas, Keltie. *Rising Seas: Flooding, Climate Change and Our New World.* 2nd ed. Buffalo: Firefly Books, 2023.
In this book, you'll get a view of what the Earth might look like under the rising sea levels of climate change. It includes side-by-side comparisons of an area's present-day with its projected future.

WEBSITES

International Union for the Conservation of Nature (IUCN)

https://www.iucn.org/

The IUCN is one of the largest environmental and conservation networks. Their website provides a library of scientific publications, status on habitat and organism populations, and resources that help governments and individuals adapt to climate change.

National Aeronautics and Space Administration (NASA)

https://science.nasa.gov/

Through the lens of atmospheric science, the NASA website provides easy-to-understand climate change science and educational resources.

National Oceanographic and Atmospheric Administration (NOAA)

https://www.noaa.gov/

The NOAA website hosts climate change and atmospheric research for the public, including many resources on climate adaptation strategies.

United Nations Framework Convention on Climate Change (UNFCCC): Adaptation Knowledge Portal

https://www4.unfccc.int/sites/nwpstaging/Pages/Home.aspx

The UNFCCC website provides conference summaries, climate change news articles, climate action resources, and updates on upcoming climate change meetings and events around the world. Find articles and resources on climate adaptation through this portal.

US Environmental Protection Agency (EPA): Climate Adaptation Plans

https://www.epa.gov/climate-adaptation/climate-adaptation-plans

The EPA seeks to protect US natural resources and human health. They focus on assessing, monitoring, and improving land, air, and water quality. On this page, they offer tips for forming and enacting climate adaptation plans.

INDEX

adaptation, 4–5, 10, 13–23, 28–41, 43–55
adaptation fund, 41
adaptation plans, 11, 20, 33, 43–47, 49, 52
adaptive capacity, 13–14, 17, 34, 43
apex predators, 26
Arctic fox, 5–6

behavioral adaptation, 5, 28, 38
biodiversity, 26, 28, 32, 38

carbon capture, 31, 36
carbon capture and storage, 24
carbon tax policy, 35
Climate Action Network (CAN), 42
climate change, 4, 6–35, 37–55
climate change adaptation, 8–15
climate change risks, 4
climate models, 9
climate-monitoring technologies, 43
climate-resilient development, 41
climate-smart policies, 53
coastal erosion, 25
coastal towns, 4
community adaptation, 47–50
Conference of Parties (COP), 41
coral bleaching, 30

deforestation, 26, 55
diversion canals, 20

ecosystems, 24, 27, 32, 38
ectotherms, 29, 32
emperor penguins, 5
Environmental Protection Agency (EPA), 44
erosion, 25, 38, 49
Eunice Newton Foote, 9
extinction, 6, 26, 28, 32

financial resources, 19–21, 41
flood barriers, 20
Flood risk planning, 19
floods, 7, 26, 47–48
food security, 16, 21
forest fires, 32
fossil fuels, 6, 36, 41, 52

glacial melting, 30
Glasgow Climate Pact, 41
global warming, 6, 32
golden toad, 6
government limitations, 21–22
Great Green Wall Africa, 38
green building code, 35
greenhouse effect, 7, 9
greenhouse gases, 26, 29
Guy Callender, 9

heat waves, 7, 23, 30, 32, 39, 47

incremental adaptation, 33
individual actions, 52
Infrastructural adaptation, 36
institutional adaptation, 35
Intergovernmental Panel on Climate Change (IPCC), 10
International Adaptation Fund, 24, 41, 43

kelp forests, 26
knowledge gap, 22, 25

landslides, 38, 49

maladaptation, 19, 23–24
mangroves, 32
mitigation, 13

natural disasters, 7, 26
nature-based solutions, 24, 37

ocean heat waves, 30

proactive adaptation, 35
Productive Safety Net Program (PSNP), 16

renewable energy sources, 36
resilience, 13–16, 32
rising sea levels, 13, 34

seawalls, 25, 49
sensitivity, 15, 17
smart bins, 36
soil quality, 32, 34
solar panels, 13, 36
Southern California, 4
Svante Arrhenius, 9

transformational adaptation, 34
Tyndall, 9

United Nations Framework Convention on Climate Change (UNFCCC), 24
United Nations (UN), 10

vulnerability, 13–17, 40, 54

water-saving, 43
wind turbine farms, 36
women's empowerment, 43
World Bank, 43

ABOUT THE AUTHOR

Kayla Andra grew up in Utah. As a teenager, she developed a love for traveling, volunteering abroad, and the ocean. Some of her endeavors include sea turtle conservation in Costa Rica, elephant conservation in Thailand, sea turtle rehabilitation in Thailand, white shark research in South Africa, and, most recently, working as a SCUBA divemaster in Indonesia. Kayla has a master's degree in marine biology and has studied the effect of climate change on small-scale fisheries. She continues to travel and freelance as a Marine Biologist, aiming to educate others about the sea and inspiring them to find and follow their joy.

PHOTO ACKNOWLEDGMENTS

Clare Louise Jackson/Shutterstock, cover; SofieLion/Shutterstock, p.5; SANDIP NEOGI/Shutterstock, p.7; Erdal Sekerr/Shutterstock, p.10; Lindsey Seitz/Shutterstock, p.12; Catherine Anne Thomas/Shutterstock, p.14; Riccardo Mayer/Shutterstock, p.16; corlaffra/Shutterstock, p.18; CrackerClips Stock Media/Shutterstock, p.20; Riccardo Mayer/Shutterstock, p.22; Oksana Bali/Shutterstock, p.24; CassandraSm/Shutterstock, p.27; Aaryan_Mishra/Shutterstock, p.29; Kavishka_Creator/Shutterstock, p.30; yatharthag/Shutterstock, p.31; Fotokostic/Shutterstock, p.34; pixelheadphoto digitalskillet/Shutterstock, p.36; travelview/Shutterstock, p.37; Petronelka/Shutterstock, p.39; Vitpho/Shutterstock, p.42; RagabGamal/Shutterstock, p.44; Michael Siluk/Shutterstock, p.45; Bandersnatch/Shutterstock, p.47; Jonathan A. Mauer/Shutterstock, p.49; Mike Workman/Shutterstock, p.51; Jacob Lund/Shutterstock, p.53; yvonnestewarthenderson/Shutterstock, p.55